Knowledge

Change

Acceptance

Possibilities

Keeping track of resources, concerns, milestones, breakthroughs,notes, releasing your worries is so beneficial. Sometimes it can be hard to see the light at the end of the tunnel, especially after a hard day or episode.
<u>Always remember:</u>
At the end of the day you made it, that alone is success!

I am a mother to a child with special needs who was diagnosed at a very young age with multiple diagnoses. I help children and families through my career as a Child Development Specialist/ Behaviorist in Early Intervention. I am a Board certified Cognitive Specialist (BCCS) and also a Certified Autism Travel Professional (CATP). Making this my life 24/7. I understand what it is like to feel walls closing in, unsure what to do next, how to be there for your child, and how to assist others in understanding your child.

Labels DO NOT set limitations!

Thank you for purchasing this notebook.
– *Nicole*

www. Autismangles.Com

This Book
Belongs to:

____

Knowledge
IS POWER

Knowledge
CREATES CHANGE

Change
MOVES TO ACCEPTANCE

Acceptance
LEADS TO POSSIBILITIES

Believe
IN YOUR CHILD & YOURSELF!

You Are Not Alone!

www.ingramcontent.com/pod-product-compliance
Lightning Source LLC
Chambersburg PA
CBHW061719250726
48657CB00002B/687